JOURNAL

OF

A TOUR TO THE WHITE MOUNTAINS

IN JULY, 1784

By JEREMY BELKNAP, D.D.

Accompanied with a Map

Printed from the Original Manuscript, with a Prefatory Note by the Editor

BOSTON
MASSACHUSETTS HISTORICAL SOCIETY
1876

JOURNAL

OF

A TOUR TO THE WHITE MOUNTAINS

IN JULY, 1784

By JEREMY BELKNAP, D.D.

Printed from the Original Manuscript, with a Prefatory
Note by the Editor

BOSTON
MASSACHUSETTS HISTORICAL SOCIETY
1876

From the " Belknap Papers," published by the Massachusetts Historical Society.

PREFATORY NOTE.

Dr. Belknap's account of his tour to the White Mountains, in July, 1784, is here printed from his original note-book, in the form of a diary, preserved in the cabinet of this Society. The narrative, or text, is written on the right-hand pages of the manuscript, and occasional remarks, some of them perhaps subsequently written, on the left. The greater part of these latter might have been introduced into the text, but we have preferred to let them stand as written, and have printed them here as foot-notes. The abbreviated words, which abound in the manuscript, have generally been spelled out at length, and a proper punctuation introduced, which, in the rough notes, was not always regarded by the writer.

The several mountains known as the White Mountain group, the central cluster, had not been named at the time Dr. Belknap made this visit. Eight years later, as early certainly as 1792, the highest peak had been named "Mount Washington."

In the third volume of Dr. Belknap's History of New Hampshire, published in 1792, he gives a description of the White Mountains, and refers to the visit made to them by a party of gentlemen in 1784; but he gives no intimation that he was one of the party. A similar description, previously written, had been communicated to the American Philosophical Society, at Philadelphia, and was printed, but without his consent, in the second volume of their Transactions, in 1786. Both these accounts, quite different in form from the Journal we here produce, contain additional particulars.

Of three of the gentlemen who accompanied Dr. Belknap, it may be added that the Rev. Daniel Little was minister of the church in Kennebunk, Me., then included in the township of Wells; the Rev. Manassah Cutler, of Ipswich, was an early member of the Historical Society, one of the projectors of the Ohio Company, and distinguished through life for his scientific attainments, particularly in the department of botany; Dr. Joshua Fisher, of Beverly, was a distinguished physician and naturalist, President of the Massachusetts Medical Society, and founder of a professorship in Harvard College. All these gentlemen were members of the American Academy of Arts and Sciences.

This journey was made on horseback. Going up in the direction of Bartlett and Jackson, the party entered the defile now known as the "Pinkham Notch;" and, after having pitched their tent on the high ground between the Ellis and Peabody Rivers, prepared to ascend the great mountain on foot. Returning from this excursion, they proceeded on in the same direction as far as Dartmouth (now Jefferson), where they were refreshed at the plantation of Colonel Whipple, who had joined their party at Conway. Staying over one day, they set out the next morning on their return; passed over a part of Pondicherry Mountain, crossed the river Amonoosuck, and arrived at the Western Notch, the source of the Saco River, through which they proceeded on their homeward way, making a complete circuit of the central group of the White Mountains.

The earliest recorded ascent of the White Mountains was made in 1642, by "one Darby Field, an Irishman, living about Pascataquack, being accompanied with two Indians." They "went to the top of the White Hill. He made his journey in 18 days." This is the language of Governor Winthrop in his History (II. 67), who has recorded the interesting details. This visit, or the record of it, was made in the month of June. Field repeated his visit "about a month after." A few months later, Winthrop notices another visit, made by Thomas Gorges and Richard Vines: "They went up Saco River in birch canoes, and, that way, they found it 90 miles to Pegwaggett, an Indian town; but, by land, it is but 60." They seem, also, to have ascended the principal mountain. "They went and returned in 15 days." (Ibid. 89.)

John Josselyn, who made a visit to New England in 1638, and again in 1663, and published two books about the country, describes the White Mountains in a way a visitor to them would write; but, as he does not speak of having made the journey himself, he may have derived his information from others. He mentions some particulars not described by Winthrop. His account was printed in his "New England's Rarities" published in London in 1672.

From this time to that of Dr. Belknap's visit, these

mountains had been frequently ascended, by ranging parties; but no adequate description of them had been written. Dr. Cutler preserved some notes of this tour, as appears by a quotation from them by Dr. Belknap in one of his accounts of the mountains.

Dr. Jacob Bigelow visited the mountains in the summer of 1816, and published an excellent description of them in the New England Journal of Medicine and Surgery, Vol. V. p. 321–338. Since then numerous accounts have appeared. This *whole region* has become a favorite resort for summer retreat, as the Switzerland of New England; and numerous guide-books, including the luxurious volume of the late Thomas Starr King, abound in descriptions of every group. A good map of the mountains, and the country surrounding them, is still a *desideratum*.

The computations made by Dr. Belknap's party as to the heights of the several mountains have since been shown to be erroneous.

The very few foot-notes made by the editor, while this journal was passing through the press, bear the distinguishing mark.

C. D.

CAMBRIDGE, MASS., May 10, 1876.

NOTE TO MAP.

THE map which accompanies this journal is a *fac-simile* of one drawn by Dr. BELKNAP at the time, or rather copied by him from a plan in possession of Mr. WHIPPLE, of Dartmouth, one of his companions on the route. This appears from the following extract from his letter to Mr. Hazard, of 19 Aug., 1784: —

"For your farther gratification, I have copied a plan which I took from one in Mr. Whipple's possession, shewing the course of the rivers and the situation of part of the mountains. His plan extended no farther north, so that the northern part of our circuit and his plantation are not comprehended in it. I have added the sketches of the appearance of the mountains on the east and the north-west, and marked their area as nearly as I could. The roads in which we travelled are marked with a pricked line."

Dr. BELKNAP's map was sketched or copied with a *pen* as to the delineation of the rivers, &c., with their names and the names of the mountains; but "the appearance of the mountains" and "their area" were indicated with a *lead pencil*. These pencil marks are represented in the map herewith by stippling, or dots.

DR. BELKNAP'S
TOUR TO THE WHITE MOUNTAINS.

Tuesday, July 20, 1784. Set out from home on a tour to the White Mountains, &c., in company with Rev. Mr. Little, of Wells, Mr. Cutler, of Ipswich, Dr. Fisher, of Beverly, Mr. Heard, of Ipswich, and two young gentlemen, Hubbard and Bartlet, from College. Got to Rochester. Wind, W.

Wednesday, July 21. At a quarter after 7, set out from Rochester. Dined at Copps's, in Wakefield. The upper part of Wakefield well settled. About 4 miles above Copps's descended a steep hill, and came to a large brook, which vents into Pine River, a branch of great Ossapy. *Crossed an old beaver dam* on another branch of said brook. Passed over a mountain in New Garden, Seagel's hill, from whence we had a very grand opening to the N., presenting to view distant ridges of very high mountains, rising behind each other, the farthest supposed to be the White Mountains; but, the air being hazy, could not certainly determine. Wind, S.E.

Distance, 32 miles from Rochester Old Hill to Brown's, at N. Garden, where we stopt.

Joined company at Rochester; Mr. Enoch Wingate and Mr. George Place.

Thursday, July 22. Set out from Brown's. Seven and one-half miles from thence to Great Ossapy Pond, 5 miles in length, and nearly round. Pine River comes into the south part of it. *The Ossapy River runs out of the pond, first northerly, then turns easterly, under a large* *mountain in Effingham,* formerly called Seven Mountain; now Green Mountain.*

Lovel's fort at the north side of this great Pond, near a small stream.

Rode through pitch pine 7 miles, to Eaton. Dined at Dr. Jackson's. Corua † and White-face Mountains on the left.

Crossed Little Pigwacket River (stopped at Abbot's), then Saco Swift River, then Saco Main River, and got to McMillan's at sunset. ‡

25 miles distance to-day. Found Mr. Whipple § and Mr. Evans ready to go with us. ||

Friday, July 23. At quarter past eight, A.M., set off for the White Mountains. When advanced about 7 or 8 miles, had a full front view of the great Mountain,¶ which appeared like a naked rock, of its proper grey color, inclining to brown, the channels where water descends plainly discernible, being whiter than the rest. Crossed the E. branch of Saco River, and the E. branch of Ellis River. Rode up the Mountains, by Ellis's River, which runs down a long descent, and is almost one continued fall. About 10 got to Copps's, the last house; ** took some refreshment, and proceeded along the old Shelburne road, full of windfalls and mires, and overgrown with bushes. About 4

---

* Crossed Pine River, current N.W., about 4 miles before we came to Ossapy bridge.

† Chocorua. — ED.

‡ At Conway. — ED.

On Esq. Merrill's farm the remains of 2 Indian stockade forts.

Esq. McMillan assured me there was snow remaining on the White Mountains, S. side, within 10 days past; the like was told me by Mr. Abbot; both of Conway.

We had, at McMillan's, full-grown cucumbers. At Brown's, last night, new potatoes, about one-half grown.

§ Col. Joseph Whipple, of Dartmouth, now Jefferson. — ED.

|| Our pilot, Captain Evans, assured me that when he was on the Mountain, June 19, 1774, the snow was 5 feet deep in one spot near the summit of the Mountain; and that a fortnight before that, some of the people who were then at work with him on Shelburne road, found it 13 feet deep in the same spot.

¶ Subsequently called Mount Washington. — ED.

** In Jackson. — ED.

o'clock got to the *New River*, which broke forth in 1775; it forms a cascade of upwards of 100 feet, visible at its descent into Ellis River, and has borne down rocks, trees, before it. I ascended above 100 feet, and some of the company higher; the cascade is varied and winding, in some places confined within 2 feet, in others forming a wide sheet, and on some flat rocks a bason.

Three-fourths of a mile further brought us to our proposed encamping ground, which is near a meadow, in which Ellis's River and a branch of Amariscogin have their heads; consequently, we are on the height of land between Saco and Amariscogin waters. Here we turned our horses into the meadow, and built a hut* of poles and bark, with an hemlock bed; and, having made a good fire before it, retired to rest. This day fair and cool.

Saturday, July 24. A fine morning. After breakfast, and due preparations, began to ascend the Mountain from the eastern side, our course about N.W. At the first steep ascent, Dr. F., finding a pain in his side, which disabled him, returned to the camp, where Mr. Whipple's negro man attended to take care of the horses and baggage. We then ascended about 2 hours, keeping a large stream which runs off the Mountain into Ellis River on our left.† Having risen many very steep and extremely difficult precipices, I found my breath fail; and, the company having been obliged to make many pauses on my account, and the pilot supposing we were not more than half way to the Plain, a consultation was held, and it was thought best that I should return before we proceeded further.

---

* While the hut was building, I walked into the meadow with Mr. Little, and took a view of the Mountain, which appeared in two very high peaks and several ridges, one of which was bare. Mr. Whipple, desiring to set the Mountain with the compass, I went again with him, and fell into a deep hole full of water up to my hips; returned and shifted as well as I could, but received so much damage from this accident that I was ill all night; feverish and weak.

† This stream we called *Cutler's River*. We also saw a *brook with a frothy scum*, which, on tasting, proved to be saponaceous.

Two of the gentlemen offered to be my company; but, thinking it would deprive them of the pleasure they expected to reap from ascending the Mountain, I concluded to come down alone, keeping the stream on my right. In about an hour and half I got on level ground, and my voice was heard at the camp, where I arrived, I suppose, about 10 o'clock, much fatigued; took some refreshment, and went to sleep.*

Saturday, P.M. Went with Dr. F. into the meadow, and examined a beaver dam, under which the water runs N. into Amariscogin branch; and, at a little distance out of the same meadow, it runs S. into Ellis River. The Dr. saw a blue bird, with a white head, which is said to be a *saw-whetter*, alias *carrion-bird*. As it grew toward night, we secured the horses, picked up wood for our fire, and, it beginning to rain, repaired our tent with bark, took all the baggage into it, anxiously expecting the return of our friends, but they appeared not; we therefore went to rest. The rain increased, and continued all night. Our tent leaked, and our fire decayed; but, by frequent attention, we kept it alive, and so continued to lay as that we avoided being wet.

Sunday, July 25. At daylight it ceased raining.† Our anxiety about our friends was partly removed by hearing the report of a gun, which we answered; it was repeated by them once, and by us twice, and they presently after

---

* In my descent saw and came down *one precipice completely perpendicular, the stones faced and laid as* regular *as a wall of hewn stone,* 4 *or* 5 *feet high and* 7 *or* 8 *rods long.*

The rocks covered with green moss, and the interstices filled with it, so as to bear our weight, though it gave way under our feet; in some places we slipped through.

Instruments brought out: 2 barometers, 2 thermometers, 1 sextant, 1 telescope, 2 surveying compasses, 1 chain. 1 barometer broke before we got to the Mountains. 1 thermometer rendered useless after we left the Mountains. 1 compass broke, the other barometer broke. These accidents were unavoidable, considering the rough ways we passed through, the rubs and knocks we endured in the woods; though, happily, no person received any greater damage than a broken shin.

† Insects very troublesome this morning.

arrived safe, having been obliged to pass the night on the Mountain, round a fire which they kindled, and which was their only defence against the rain. They had ascended to the summit, but had not so good a view as they wished, the Mountain being most of the time involved in clouds, which rolled up, and down, and in every direction, above, below, and around them. After I left them, the ascent became much more steep and difficult, the growth shorter and shorter, till it came to shrubs, then short bushes, then a sort of grass called winter grass, mixed with moss. The bushes are either fir or spruce. A sort of red berry and blue berry grow on small vines.

The Plain is composed of stones, covered with moss mixed with this winter grass; the moss of a light grey colour (that below is *green*), and so spread over the stones and their interstices as to look like the surface of a dry pasture or common (in some parts the interstices of the rocks were filled with moss; in others, open and dry). In some openings,* water appeared. The area of this Plain is an irregular figure, supposed near a mile from the edge to the bottom of the pinnacle.* Sugar loaf is a pile of loose, dark grey rocks, supposed about 100 † feet per-

---

* The clouds prevented their view of the Plain on the W. side, so that they could not determine its extent that way.

† Afterwards, judging by some eminences which they measured, Mr. Cutler and the rest were satisfied the height of this pinnacle [was] not less than 300 feet; but I suspect it is at least 1000, or it would make no figure at all on such an elevated plain.

	h. m.
From the time of leaving the tent till their arrival at the top of the pinnacle	6 51
Stops deducted	1 38
	5 13
Walking from the 1st summit over the plain to the 2d, or highest	1 21

They set out from the tent at 15 m. after 6 A.M., and arrived at the 2d summit at 1.6 P.M.

Left the pinnacle at	3 57
Descended a precipice; returned and came by the 1st summit; left it at	5 50
Entered the woods	6 33
Encamped by a fire	8
Arrived the next morning at the tent	6 6
I left the company on my return, at	8 20

pendicular height, and not so difficult of ascent as the precipice below the Plain, which, in some places, is inaccessible; especially on the S.E. side; on the E. side they went up. (The degree of heat on the thermometer at the top of the Mountain was more than when they left the tent.) But the exercise of ascending so heated them, that when they came to rest on the top of the Mountain, they felt a coldness in the air which made them shiver like a frosty night in October. The weather was so thick that they could not observe the latitude, though a sextant was carried for the purpose. They cut the letters N. H. on the uppermost rock, and the letters of their names, with a chisel.

After breakfast, Mr. C. went into the meadow and took a base and angles to measure the height of that part of the top of the Mountain visible from thence, which is not the highest pinnacle, but a bluff on the eastern side of the Plain; then, mounting our horses, we set out, about 9 o'clock, for Mr. Whipple's plantation, at Dartmouth;* proceeded down Peabody River, keeping it on our left, after having crossed it near its source. This is the Shelburne road, which has not been travelled for some years, and is grown up with bushes and filled with wind-falls, the bridges broke, and the mires deep. After travelling about 6 miles, at 1 o'clock we found the road cut off by the River, which, in some violent flood, had changed its course more to the E., leaving the old channel on the opposite side dry, as far as we could see. Here we sat down and dined, while our pilot went back to reconnoitre, and soon returned, reporting that the place where we should have crossed the river was about 100 rods back. We then went back, crossed the River, and took another old road, which had once been cut, but was now filled, and travelled with much difficulty, at the rate of a mile and a half an hour,

---

* Now Jefferson. — ED.

one going before with an ax. Met with a shower, which wet us to the skin; found ourselves deceived as to the distance, and were obliged to encamp in the woods, and turn our horses out to browse the bushes. This P.M. we crossed another branch of Amariscogin River,* called *Moose River*.

Monday, July 26. After an uncomfortable night, we were so happy as to find our horses at a small distance from our hut, and proceeded on our journey, supposing ourselves within 8 miles of Mr. W.'s plantation, and that we had rode about 18 miles the day before. Along this road yesterday and this morning we saw the culheags, or log-traps, which the hunters set for sables. They are composed of 2 sticks of about 4 or 5 inches diameter, and 10 or 12 feet long, one side of each made smooth so as to shut close one upon the other; a semicircular inclosure of long chips of wood set in the ground, about a foot in diameter and 2 feet high, covered with bushes; the logs are laid on the open side of this semicircle, and set apart by a small stick about 4 inches long, picked at the lower end, which is set on another horizontal stick, flat on the upper side and round underneath; this is also pointed at one end, where the bait is placed; two other chips are set without the logs to keep them steady, so as the upper one may fall directly on the lower one. The space between the traps is scented by drawing a piece of meat on the ground; the sable is thereby guided to the trap, and, putting his head into the hole between the logs, which is the only place where he can come at it, the motion of pulling out the bait springs the trap, and catches him by the head, or neck, or back.

After riding four hours and a half, and being overtaken with another shower, having crossed the height of land

---

* In the branches of Amariscogin which we crossed this day I observed a great number of *tad-poles*; there was *in Moose River and in a branch of Israel River wild oats*, which our horses snapt at greedily.

between Moose River and Israel River, and forded the latter and a branch of it, we came to some old felled trees and got to Mr. W.'s opening. Had a full view of the Mountains covered with clouds, and got into a road which brought us to his house.

His plantation is situated on the intervals formed by Israel's River. The summit of the White Mountains bears S.E. from his house. Here we rested and were refreshed after a most tedious journey through the wilderness.

About 2 miles off is a pond where the moose at this season go to bathe, to get clear of the flies, and are sometimes shot in the water. Mr. W. has a pair of moose horns which extend four and a half feet and weigh thirty-four pounds.

Mr. Hight, who lives on Mr. Whipple's place, told me he had seen snow on the N.W. side of the White Mountains within 3 weeks past.*

From here, as the road goes, 11 miles to the nearest part of Connecticut River, in Northumberland.

The land we passed through yesterday, between Peabody River and Israel River, is called *Durand;* some of it very good.

Tuesday, July 27. Cloudy on the Mountains. About

---

* This information I believe was mistaken, and that instead of 3, he should have said 5 weeks. I have reason to think, however, and was so informed, that the snow lies longer on the S. side, where it is seen at Conway, than on the N. or N.W. side. The N.W. wind blows it over the tops of the mountains, and drives it into the long deep vallies or gullies, where it is formed into a very hard body, 20 or 40 feet deep or more.

Remark. If so vast a quantity of snow lodges and remains on the White Mountains, how many more mountains are there towards the N.W. whose frozen summits give the keenness to the wind. 'Tis not the lakes nor the forests that make the N.W. winds so piercing, but the hoary tops of infinite ranges of mountains, some of which, at the remotest regions, may retain the snow undissolved through the year.

The long green moss on the steep sides of the Mountains serves as a sponge to retain the vapors which are brought by the winds in the form of clouds against these Mountains, and there deposited; it also preserves the rain-water from running off at once, and keeps the springs supplied with a perpetual dripping.

10 o'clock clears up for about half an hour, so that we had a distinct view of the N.W. side of the White's 7 summits, ranging N.E. and S.W., the heads of 4 or 5 of them bald. From the accounts I have collected from near observers, as well as my own observations, have no doubt remaining that the *sole* cause of the bright appearance which these Mountains make is the *snow* which falls on their bald summits every year as early as September and goes not wholly off till July. The rocks of which the summits are composed are a *dark grey* covered with a yellowish moss; the appearance at the distance of 10 or 15 miles is brown, excepting some streaks, which, at some seasons, are water-courses; these are of a lighter color, and are plainly discernible with the naked eye to differ from the other parts. There are also dark streaks, which, through the telescope, are seen to be the shaded sides of the long winding and deep valleys which are on every side of the Mountains.

This P.M. a thunder shower. The people of this place, who are 5 or 6 families, assembled in Mr. Whipple's barn, and I preached them a sermon, the first ever preached here, from 1 Cor. 6: 19, 20. Mr. Little baptized 8 of their children. Mr. Cutler made the concluding prayer. 38 people of the place were present, and seemed pleased with the attention paid them.*

We attempted to take the height and distance of several of the neighboring Mountains, but they were so obscured by the clouds passing over and rising on them that we were obliged to desist.

---

* As we passed through Eaton and Conway, the appearance of so many people, more than ever had been seen at once travelling that way, was very amusing to the people. We had 3 guns and 1 pair of pistols in the company. The barometers were slung across the back of one, and the sextant was carried in a large bag. This uncommon appearance was the subject of much speculation; and the good women, understanding there were 3 ministers in the company, were in hopes we should *lay the spirits* which have been supposed to hover about the White Mountains, an opinion very probably derived from the Indians, who thought these Mountains the habitation of some invisible beings, and never attempted to ascend them.

Wednesday, July 28. Six o'clock, morning, set out on our return, leaving Dr. Fisher behind, who is collecting birds and other animal and vegetable productions. Passed over part of Pondicherry Mountain, and about quarter past 11 arrived at the Western Notch of the Whites, having crossed Amonoosuck and its branches several times, and seen a bear-trap on the road, constructed like the culheags, but larger and stronger. At the Notch a meadow, through which a brook runs into Saco River. This meadow, surrounded on all sides with mountains, some of them perpendicular, is a singularly romantic and picturesque scene.*
Mr. Cutler took an observation to ascertain the latitude. The narrowest part of this passage I measured, from one perpendicular rock to the other, and is 22 feet. The direction of the defile N. and S.; on the W. side runs the brook. The Eastern is formed into a causeway and road with great labor and expense; it was formerly only a rough watercourse, and not known till, about 13 years ago, two hunters passed through it; † soon after which the proprietors of land at the Upper Cohass formed a plan for a road through it, the only practicable pass through these Mountains to the upper settlements on Connecticut River; distance, 25 miles from Northumberland or Lancaster. The proceeds of a confiscated estate, W. Stark's, ‡ have been applied, £400, toward making this road, which, for 100 rods or more down the southern side and along by the meadow on the top, is a work of great labor. Two streams come down the eastern side of this defile, forming beautiful cascades. One of

---

* The most romantic imagination here finds itself surprized and stagnated. Every thing which it had formed an idea of as sublime and beautiful is here realized. Stupendous mountains, hanging rocks, chrystal streams, verdant woods, the cascade above, the torrent below, all conspire to amaze, to delight, to soothe, to enrapture; in short, to fill the mind with such ideas as every lover of nature and every devout worshipper of its Author would wish to have.

† Nash and Sawyer. — ED.

‡ Col. William Stark, a brother of Gen. John, the hero of Bennington. He was one of the proprietors of Fryeburg. He joined the British at the Revolution, and his estate was confiscated. — ED.

them is so narrow as exactly to resemble a flume, and goes by that name. These run under bridges in the road, and wind away down its western side into Saco River. For 2 miles from the summit of this romantic pass the Mountains on each side rise almost, and in some places quite, perpendicular, and shew several bare and whitish rocks with polished sides, totally inaccessible. Some of these, especially when crusted over with ice, may have given rise to the fable of the *Carbuncle,* with the help of a little imagination and the reflection of the moon or star beams.

The Mountains continue on each side of the road at the distance of not more than a mile, and, in some places, not so much, for a long way, 8 or 10 miles from the Notch; and Saco River runs between them. This River is well known to rise and fall very quick; its descent is rapid and full of falls. Passed by Sawyer's Rock, down which last summer a moose fell, and 2 men who saw him cut his hamstrings and his throat with a pocket-knife. Several of the branches of Saco River are now entirely dry. In one place the river threatens to cut off the road and change its course, as it has done before. At night got to Enoch Emery's,* and lodged there.†

Thursday, July 29. Breakfasted at McMillan's, ‡ parted with Mr. Cutler and company, and, with Mr. Little, proceeded toward Fryeburg. Dined with Mr. Porter. After-

---

* In Bartlett. — ED.

† We encompassed the White Mountains in riding about 70 miles, and, considering the distance at which we were from them in some part of the compass, we judged the base of the Mountains would not be less than an area of 50 miles. The peaks or summits within this space we could not enumerate; but all this body may properly be called one ridge or cluster of mountains, and the range extends N.E. and S.W. to an unknown distance. The form of this cluster which we encompassed seems to be about the form of an isosceles triangle, whose longest extremity is toward the S.

Observed as we came along that the people made little smokes in their cowyards to defend their cows against the flies and mosquitoes.

‡ In Conway. — ED.

noon rode to Fryeburg; visited Lovel's Pond, the scene of a memorable battle with the Indians in 1725. Lovel's march from Great Ossapy, which is not more than 20 or 22 miles, brought him to the W. side of this Pond, where he saw, on a rocky point of land opposite, the distance of a mile or more, an Indian fishing, with a fowling-piece with which he had just before fired at some ducks. He was not set for a decoy, and has no pretensions to the character of an hero, as has been represented. To come at him they had to march 2 or 3 miles round the N.E. end of the Pond. They met him returning to the Indian fort, about 1 and a half miles from the Pond; he fired and wounded Lovel, and they killed him. They had left their packs on the pitch pine land at the N.E. end of the Pond. While they were gone after this Indian, 2 companies of Indians under Captains Paugus and Nathaniel, who had been down Saco River and were returning, came on their track and followed them to where they had left their packs, which they seized, and by that means found their number 34; their own, 41. (This account I had from Evans, who had it from one of the Indians that was in the fight.) They then lay in ambush for them among the brakes and wind-falls and shrub oaks on the pitch pine plain adjoining the Pond; and, when Lovel's men returned to where they had left their packs, the Indians rose and fired on both sides of them. Lovel and some others were killed; the rest, thinking to secure themselves, retreated (through a bog of 2 or 3 rods width and 12 or 14 long) to the sandy beach of the Pond, hoping to screen themselves behind the trees which grew to the water's edge, or some rising near the beach.*

The place where they retreated is singularly situated. The Pond was in their rear, which here forms a cove; in their front was a bog; on their right, a brook, then un-

---

* The Indians immediately drew off from Pigwacket, and left their own dead unburied, and ours not scalped.

fordable; on their left, a rocky point; from this point, and from the bushes beyond the brook, the Indians enfiladed them, and fired at them from behind the bog. The beach being only a level sand, they were exposed on every side. A few pitch pine trees stood between the bog and the water; but these could afford them no shelter, as the enemy were on three sides of them. The trees still retain the marks of the balls, and the letters of the names of the dead who were buried here. It is astonishing that the Indians ever left the ground, as they had this company completely in their power, there being no possibility of their escape. Their situation was to the greatest degree hazardous and forlorn; more so than can be conceived by any person who has not visited the spot.

Major Osgood told me he was one of a party who helped to run the Province line, some years ago, — the 60 miles end at the edge of the interval on Captain Brown's land. They then measured 24 miles to Amariscogin, and 16 miles beyond; 40 in all. I. R.,* who had the direction, would not go farther, because their bread was out, though they had that morning killed a fine moose, and offered to proceed without bread. The end of the 40 miles is on high land, supposed within four miles of Umbagog Lake and in sight; the line would cross it. Shelburne lies 3 miles S. and 3 miles N. of Amariscogin.

Captain Evans told me he lived at Penacook in the Cape Breton war, and that 5 men were killed there in *August*, 1747. The Indians had intended to attack the people in the meeting-house; but, seeing some of them go armed to meeting, were afraid. The next morning they waylaid the road and killed these men, who were going to N. Hopkinton; two months after killed another, who had just returned from 2 years' absence at Cape Breton; one at Suncook.

---

* Isaac Rindge, who surveyed this line in 1768. — ED.

Grindstones are found at Fryeburg and at Amariscogin, of a fine grit, and hard; will do very well for small tools, and, with the help of rifle-sand strewed on them wet, will grind an ax. Captain Brown, at whose house I put up, has one.

Friday, July 30. At half past six set out with Mr Little from Fryeburg, and rode through Brown's field, chiefly pitch pine land. About 10 o'clock got to the great falls in Saco River. About half a mile above them are 3 hills, and between the hills and the river 2 meadows, a ridge of land between them, over which the road passes. The meadows have a communication by a brook. These hills, I suppose, are Sunday's Rocks. The land not good; pitch pine, mixed with white oak and whortleberry bushes. The falls we judged not more than 40 feet perpendicular, though the descent may be as many rods. Up these falls the salmon cannot go, by reason of a rock at the bottom, which projects; they therefore pass up the Great Ossapy River, on which is the remains of an Indian weir, built with stones and wood, for taking them. We crossed this river about noon; our horses swam after a canoe, in which we put our saddles and bags; an old woman paddled us over. Got some dinner on the other side, at the house of one Thompson. From thence 12 miles to the Little Ossapy, the land is extremely good, beech and maple; the lower part of the way well settled, good farms, plenty of grass and grain; the place is called Limerick. In the evening got to Massabesick;* crossed Little Ossapy on a bridge. Lodged at Captain Smith's.

Saturday, July 31. Parted with Mr. Little at Smith's. Got Mr. Burley to pilot me across the meadow and woods 3 miles to Mr. Bunker's; breakfasted there, baptized a child of Gideon Walker, visited Jo. Hamilton, got to Sanford at dinner time; dined Emery's; rode from thence

---

* Now Waterborough, in York County, Maine. — Ed.

in company with a man from Saco whose wife had run away with the Shakers and carried off 25 of his dollars; he is going in pursuit of her; got home well, about sunset.

Stages and Distances Travelled.

	Miles.	
To Rochester	8	
New Garden	32	
Ossapy Great Pond	7½	
Conway line	13	
McMillan's	4	
Height of Land	18	
		82½
To the place where we crossed Peabody River	6	
To Whipple's	20	
the Notch	14	
McMillan's	20	
		60
Fryeburg	8	
Great Ossapy	20	
Little Ossapy	12	
Captain Smith's	7	
Bunker's	3	
Dowty's Falls	17	
Dover	14	
		81
		223

Printed in Dunstable, United Kingdom